The Spiritual Teaching *of* Higher Self Yoga

The Spiritual Teaching *of* Higher Self Yoga

Nanette V. Hucknall

Published by Inner Journey Publishing,
a division of
Higher Self Yoga, Inc.

Copyright © 2021 Higher Self Yoga, Inc.
All rights reserved.

ISBN: 978-0-9894682-9-9

This book, its contents and exercises, and the author's opinions are solely for informational and educational purposes. The author specifically disclaims all responsibility for any liability, loss, or risk, personal or otherwise, which is incurred as a consequence, directly or indirectly, of the use and application of any of the contents of this book.

Dedicated to my spiritual teachers:

RHH and MM

In love and gratitude.

Table of Contents

Introduction

Many of you are new to this teaching, and some of you may want to learn more of what would be considered the esoteric material that focuses on striving for God Consciousness.

This guide will help you determine if Higher Self Yoga is the right teaching for you. It is a practical guide that discusses all the aspects of this teaching in which you will be required to participate. It also gives you an understanding about the community of Higher Self Yoga and how important it is to become a part of a sister- and brotherhood of people who are working together to achieve their spiritual goals.

Rather than say he or she throughout the book, in odd-number chapters I use he and in even-number chapters I use she, but of course the material applies to both genders.

Part One

Is Higher Self Yoga Your Spiritual Path?

Too often someone thinks that he wants to be in an esoteric teaching, but when he begins the path and is confronted with obstacles, he turns back and never follows through. Maybe in this life he is not ready to fully walk the path to the end. This is fine. In this teaching we say that someone may come and leave, but he has touched the hem of the robe, and will return in the next life, or the next, and continue. It means the person wasn't ready to meet his teacher.

One of the important things to consider in any spiritual teaching is having a teacher who has the knowledge and understanding to help you on the path. If you feel you are ready, then it is important to consider who is your destined teacher. Everyone in an esoteric teaching has a destined teacher that was given to him before he was born.

Usually the teacher is someone he has been with before, often in a different teaching that was still esoteric. If he was a Buddhist before, his teacher could have been a Lama who guided him. If he was a Hindu before, his teacher could have been his guru in the Indian tradition. Some people were in the esoteric branch of Christianity and could have had a priest for a teacher. Mainly, in all teachings that are esoteric, there have to be teachers who guide their disciples forward to achieve what they themselves have achieved.

"When a person is ready, the teacher will come." This is an old saying that is true in every esoteric religion. It means your destined teacher will appear to you, and you will know who he is when you meet him. Usually the teacher appears when you have entered an esoteric teaching, but sometimes you may find out about the teacher in an unexpected way.

There are several people in the Higher Self Yoga teaching, including the founder, who have been guided this way to their teacher.

On the other hand, some people may be interested in studying the esoteric material but not necessarily interested in choosing a teacher at that time. It is important to understand when you truly feel the need to have a teacher and when it's not right for you.

Taking the step to choose a teacher means you know fully in your heart that you are ready. Until then, it's important simply to study the teaching and learn as much as you can about what it represents.

First and foremost, the teaching must be right for you. The following are some ways you can determine whether this is true for you about Higher Self Yoga:

1. You have been doing some of the online classes, or you have been reading some of the books, and you feel the teaching is something you have enjoyed.
2. You feel what you have learned is accurate.
3. When you talk to some of the people in the teaching, you feel a sense of belonging.
4. Working with your Higher Self has helped you in your daily life.
5. The more you try to follow what the Higher Self says to you, the more you start to trust it.

6. When you feel sad or depressed, if you talk to your Higher Self, it uplifts your spirits.
7. Working with the Higher Self on practical matters has opened your desire to learn more about the spiritual aspect of Higher Self Yoga.
8. More and more, you have a desire to talk about the Higher Self to your friends.
9. If you have a loved one, you have a need to share what you have learned.
10. Mainly, your heart responds to the Higher Self teachings you have learned, and it makes you want to know and learn more.

Exercise One:

Review the ten statements above and ask yourself the following questions about each one:

1. *Can I honestly agree with this statement?*
    - *If the answer is no, ask: Why don't I agree?*
        - *Take that answer and ask:*

Does a part of me want to change this feeling?

- *If the answer is yes, ask your Higher Self: How can I do that?*

After you have gone through the ten statements, look at the ones you don't agree with, and about which you also don't want to change your feelings.

If this is true for statements two and ten, then you are not ready now to continue on to the esoteric level. This being the case, you then need to determine whether you still want to enjoy some of the things that the website offers, or you may feel that this teaching isn't the right one for you at this time.

If you feel that you still are interested in learning more about the Higher Self, then continue working with the exercises and classes.

Later, you may want to look at your answers to the above statements and see if any of them have changed. If, on the other hand, you agree with statements two and ten, then you are really interested in learning more about the Higher Self Yoga teaching. You may want to continue at a slow pace, learning how to use your Higher Self in your daily life. You also may not be ready to commit to the spiritual aspect of the teaching.

When you are ready to take that step, the following statements are ones you will agree with:

1. You can work with the Higher Self and feel it is an important part of your life.
2. You have a longing to connect to the spiritual part of Higher Self Yoga.
3. Your heart feels connected to the Higher Self, and you have a desire to fully experience its essence.
4. You know intuitively that there is more to learn, and you want to have that.
5. Sometimes you feel connected to higher realms.
6. You meditate and want to learn more about taming your thoughts.
7. You believe in reincarnation and feel there are hidden aspects of your personality that come from past lives.
8. You believe that you can grow spiritually in this teaching.
9. You want to strive and overcome the negative traits you have and develop the positive ones.
10. You believe the spiritual path of Higher Self Yoga will connect you to the Source.

If you can agree with the above statements then you are ready to look more into the esoteric teaching of Higher Self Yoga.

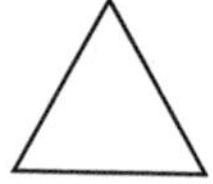

Part Two

Studying Higher Self Yoga

When a person decides to study the esoteric teaching of Higher Self Yoga, the person will need to buy some of the books that are only for that branch of the teaching. The books that are for sale in online bookstores or on the Higher Self website are the exoteric books. Two of them are still used in the esoteric part as well: *How to Live from the Heart* and *The Rose and the Sword*. There will also be two new exoteric books that will still be required reading in the esoteric branch.

It is important to speak with an elder in the teaching and find out how you can purchase the books. It is also essential to join one of the classes. The elder will suggest which class would be appropriate for you. Some of the classes have only advanced disciples in them and would be too complex for you to join.

There will also be retreats planned for new people that you would want to attend. Some of these retreats will be in person and others will be offered online. All retreats are meant to be in person, but during the pandemic are held online.

Within the community, you will meet the people who are the designated teachers. At this time, you needn't decide to work with a teacher. After you have been in the teaching longer, you may have the inner desire to further your spiritual work by having a teacher. You then will be introduced to the teachers, either online or at a physical retreat. If you are destined to have a teacher in this teaching, your heart will know who the person is.

But, again, you needn't choose a teacher if you really do not want to have one. It is very individual, and anyone entering the esoteric teaching doesn't ever have to make that decision unless the person wants to do so. Essentially, this teaching, including the spiritual aspect, can be studied by anyone who feels in her heart that it is right for her.

Once you start working in a class, you will learn how that particular class is conducted. All the leaders of the classes are disciples who have been asked to lead classes by me—the founder and leader of the Higher Self Yoga teaching—or one of the elders. I am the one who started the teaching and was given all the books. Most of the people in this teaching are my disciples.

Each class leader will decide what book to work with for the attendees. Since there is a lot of material to be studied, a new person may also want to read some of the other books privately. Every class has exercises that are done in the class, and there is a sharing process that includes feedback by all the participants. Everyone works with their Higher Self when they participate.

When you attend a retreat, there will be guidelines for you to follow, and always there will be welcoming people who will help you with logistics, etc. It is important to attend retreats because this teaching is founded on community. We are a spiritual family which not only spends time together but feels a strong bond with one another.

In the community, you will meet people for whom you have a strong feeling of friendship. Those people are usually the ones you have known in previous lives. There will also be those you instantly dislike. Obviously, they are the ones with whom you had negative past lives.

Part of the process of forming a harmonious community is to overcome those past lives that have caused the negative feelings. Realize that what has happened in a past life doesn't reflect who the person is at this time. Several other lifetimes in between have caused most people to change.

If you find you have an immediate dislike toward someone in the community, we have a process we can give you to try to understand the past and, in so doing, let those feelings go and try to move forward in the present.

Not everyone in the teaching has to love everyone else. But it is important to realize that a spiritual family is rooted in spiritual beliefs that form a basis of the spiritual family.

As in most families, there will be some you love and others with whom you simply will never feel close. The main thing is to realize that everyone shares the inner spirit within that comes from the Source.

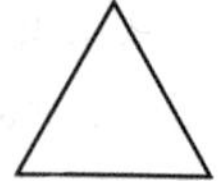

Part Three

Working with Higher Beings

Another factor in this teaching is understanding who the spiritual leaders are directing it. Most esoteric teachings work with Higher Beings who are on the subtle plane. If masculine, these beings are called Mahatmas; if feminine, they are called Taras. They are very High Initiates who have lived human lives and through their evolution have reached their present stage of enlightenment. Jesus is one of them, as is Buddha and others who have brought to humanity spiritual messages. Their responsibility is to be in charge of the evolution of this planet and of all the higher teachings that are striving to find God Consciousness.

There are also Higher Beings who direct the planetary progress according to its destined evolution as part of this solar system and its galaxy. The scientific reality of where we came from, and who we are, will in the future be discovered, but for now that reality is many years away. Some of this esoteric knowledge is given to the disciples. There is a lot that has happened in the past according to the evolutionary laws and much that is ahead of us in terms of where we will be going.

In this teaching, each student and disciple has a Mahatma or Tara who works with him. In the yoga teachings in India there are thousands of followers who are really more in the exoteric branches; but, in each one, there is an inner group of just a few people who, similar to us, are working directing with the Mahatmas and Taras. These Higher Beings help the students on their spiritual journey, and, at a certain point, when the disciple reaches a higher initiation, he then works directly with his designated Mahatma or Tara. The teacher, or what sometimes is referred to as the guru, works with the students and disciples until they reach the level where they can work directly with their Mahatma or Tara.

This happens when a disciple has achieved the fourth initiation. At that time, the disciple will become a disciple of the Mahatma or Tara and work directly with that Higher Being. This initiation gives the disciple the ability to become a teacher and have students and disciples of his own. In this teaching there are several disciples who have achieved this level. Some of them have their own students, and others are teaching the classes of my students.

When you first come into this teaching, there are mentors who can help you and answer any questions you may want to ask. These mentors are disciples in the teaching who have studied this teaching for many years. Some of them are initiates at the fourth level, and others are also advanced but not yet to that level. These mentors will be your guides and help you on your journey. Most of them are my disciples and will consult with me or an elder if you need special help or guidance.

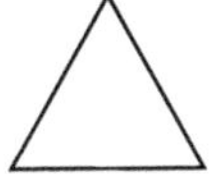

Part Four

Working with the Higher Principles

When you enter a spiritual teaching, it is important to learn its basic ideologies.

This teaching is based on developing the higher principles that constitute the Higher Self. These higher principles are within each person and are as follows:

The first principle is that of the Higher Mind. The Higher Mind is so named because it has the ability to access the Higher Wisdom that is part of the Source. This wisdom contains all the information concerning the universe and the higher laws such as the Law of Evolution. It also has access to those areas of knowledge that govern the higher worlds, or what is called the subtle planes. If a person strives to learn more about how the universe functions, the Higher Mind can tap into that knowledge. Sometimes, the Higher Mind is called the Wise Being within, because it has access to the wisdom of all that has gone before and can help a person understand more about the human journey. The Higher Self is also sometimes called the Wise Being within, because the Higher Mind is one of the principles that make up the Higher Self's contents.

The second principle is called Bhakti, which is the chalice of the heart. This contains all the positive feelings that come through the heart such as compassion, love, devotion, and comprehension of beauty. It is the chalice of fire that burns within and enlightens the beholder on the path to God Consciousness. This principle works with the Higher Mind, and the two together are linked to the higher principle called Atman, which is the seed of the person's spirit that is part of the Source.

Atman is part of each human individual. It begins to open when the person starts to question and seek to know what the Source is. When a person strives spiritually, the person will keep opening the seed and bring it into consciousness. This becomes the longing for God Consciousness and inspires someone to start the spiritual journey that will bring that person close to that understanding. The word yoga means "union with the Source," no matter what your beliefs are.

These three higher principles are all part of the Higher Self. They develop slowly as students strive and progress on their personal path.

The Higher Self is part of what is called the monad of the individual. The monad has within it all the past lives and all the characteristics of the person, both negative and positive. It is the storehouse of the individual's incarnations and brings with it some of the results of those lives, whether they were happy or sad.

Also, within the monad are desires and tendencies that have formed the individual's personality in the past. Some of those tendencies also come from hereditary genes from the person's family, but there is still an amount that comes from the individual's own monad. This is why siblings in a family differ from one another and in some cases have no similarity.

When a person is born, she brings with her the personal monad that is tied to past lives and contains the conditions of her human evolution. Usually there are additional characteristics that are acquired in a person's childhood.

There is also the strong factor of karma in families. Most people are drawn together because of their past karma with the other family members.

Unfortunately, some of this karma can be negative and cause the individual to suffer and have a difficult upbringing. But there are many who also have positive karma with their relatives and psychologically grow up healthy and strong. In this teaching, people are challenged to understand more about their past and about childhood conditioning.

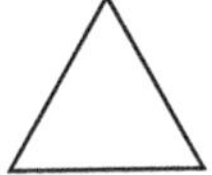

Part Five

Your Spiritual Goals

It is important that you look at what your personal goals are in a spiritual teaching. Some people really want to strive to find the Source or God, whatever your belief about the Divine consists of. Others want to learn more about how the Higher Self can help them in their daily lives, but they also want to further their understanding of how the Higher Self can help them spiritually.

Spirituality can mean many different things to different people, for instance:

1. Finding a way to open their hearts more and be more loving.
2. Learning more about the universe and evolution.
3. Understanding how science can interact with the concept of the Source or God.

4. Seeing a way to better their lives.
5. Longing to be part of a like-minded community.
6. Seeing things with the glass half empty and wanting to see things more with the glass half full.
7. Believing that they can change and grow spiritually.
8. Wanting to be more of service in the world.
9. Desiring to investigate the unknown.
10. Longing for a reality that makes better sense to them.
11. Trying to make their lives more fulfilling.
12. Believing there is more in life.
13. Seeing others in a way that helps them have faith in humankind.
14. Wanting to feel that a Higher Being is directing life.
15. Striving to find out more both personally and for the continuation of life on the planet.
16. Longing for world peace and not knowing what to do to help that happen.

17. Feeling there is more to life that they haven't yet discovered.
18. Intuiting that the what is called the Source—or God—exists and longing to find it.

All of the above can direct a person to a spiritual teaching in the hope that the teaching will give her the answers. However, a spiritual teaching of any kind, including this one, won't give you the full answers you may be longing for. It will help you find the answers yourself. It will guide you on your quest. It will not do your quest for you.

This teaching, in particular, will not tell you what you need to do. It will help lead you on your personal journey that only you can take. Each person is a unique individual. What a teacher may tell one student may completely change for another student. What's important is to know your goals and strive to fulfill them but be open to change. What your goal is today may not be your goal in five years, or ten.

It's also important to be willing to face the challenges and obstacles that can stop you along the way. Realize that each one of these will teach you something that you are meant to learn. Also, know that it will not be easy for even the most devoted or the most loving.

Exercise One

> *Look through the list of goals above and ask yourself if any of them resonate with you. Write those down, and then ask yourself if there are any other goals you have that aren't listed. Write those down.*
>
> *Put each goal in your heart and ask: How important is this goal to me at this time? Rate yourself one to ten, ten being the most important.*
>
> *When you are finished, prioritize the list, putting the most important goals at the top.*

Doing this exercise will give you a better sense of what you want to achieve in a spiritual teaching. It will also help you do the work to achieve it. Maybe some of your goals are small ones that are not at the top of your list. Look at this and maybe work with these lesser ones first. It's good to check your list of goals every month or so to see if they are still important to you. If you enter this teaching, you may find that some of the things you wanted have changed. Other goals may also come into being as you do the work. Usually, people start working toward a personal goal and later change it to a more spiritual one. You may find in time that this will happen to you.

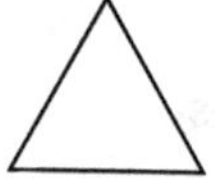

Part Six

Working with Others in the Teaching

When you come into this teaching, there may be many questions you would like to ask but feel you shouldn't do so in class because they are too basic. You may not have a strong background in the yoga tradition or even in religion per se. You also may have feelings of not wanting to appear ignorant, and even if you have a mentor, you may feel too uncomfortable to ask her. Such feelings usually come from an inner feeling of worthlessness originating in childhood. We suggest that you give these feelings to your Higher Self. Just ask it to take them away, so that you can get the answers to your questions.

The mentors all started off the same way as you. Trust that they are not judgmental and most definitely want to help you. They are doing this work of mentoring because they truly feel it's important for everyone in this teaching to have someone they can turn to for advice and understanding.

Also, if you have a question and are too embarrassed to ask it in class, just ask the teacher if you can remain for a while afterward and ask her a question. You can do the same if something was discussed in class that you didn't understand and you didn't want to say so at the time. The teachers are there to help anyone attending the classes. They are not judgmental but are advanced disciples whom you can trust will be there for you.

Sometimes a problem may arise in any class setting between two students. It's up to the teacher to try to resolve it. She may try to do so in class or choose another time to discuss it directly with the two people. If she doesn't do it in class, realize that she will do so before the next class. If you feel uncomfortable about what is happening, speak to the teacher about it.

Also, when someone works with a mentor, there may not be a good connection. If you feel you have a problem with your mentor, it's important to speak with her about it first. Then, if you feel it can't be resolved, ask me or one of the elders to assign you another mentor.

This teaching is very flexible. We want people to feel open and transparent with one another. Personalities vary and can clash. Sometimes it's because of karma, but other times it is simply a personality difference. Never stay with a mentor or even in a class if you feel this is happening with someone. There are several mentors and classes you can switch to that may be better for you.

As was said, this is a community of like-minded people who have various pasts together—some that are good and others not so good.

When you are new, what's important is to feel accepted, feel comfortable, feel you are learning what you want to learn, and feel that the people you are working with are good, caring people.

You also will be given a buddy to work with on a regular basis. It's important to do this and to share retreats and other assignments with the person—mainly material that you don't do in class.

The purpose of the buddy system is for people to have someone who can be a friend and share the teaching, other than in the class. Most buddies work together either once a week or once every two weeks. It always becomes a close relationship, especially when you get to know each other and share personal things. Everyone has enjoyed doing the buddy work. You are not required to have a buddy, but we do highly recommend that you make this part of your spiritual journey. It is helpful to be close to someone, who, like you, wants to grow spiritually.

One of the elders or I put the buddies together. Again, if you find you have difficulty with your buddy, tell me or the elder, and it will be changed.

The other area that you will participate in concerns the classes you attend. Each teacher has a class plan that is followed. You all will read a specific book and be asked to do the exercises at home. You then will share those exercises in the class setting. When you don't know the other people in the class, you may not want to share anything that is personal or related to close family members. If you feel this way, you are not required to do so. Simply say you received something you don't feel comfortable in sharing. This is also true if you go to any of the retreats, or even if you participate in a group setting on line. Your privacy is important, and you needn't share unless you want to.

Lastly, there will be times when you might want to take a break from attending classes or even doing the buddy work. If the break is just to reevaluate where you are spiritually, or how you feel about the teaching, that is perfectly fine to do. If, instead, the break is because you dislike something or someone, then it is important to talk to an elder or your mentor about what you are feeling. Sometimes doing the spiritual work and having a social life and working can seem overwhelming. It's good to cut back on the first two and adjust what you are doing, so that you will feel calm and more centered.

Everyone goes through difficult times in life. Adjusting your schedule can help give you the time you need to resolve what is happening. Be kind to yourself.

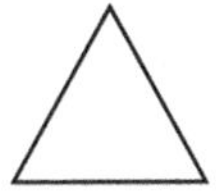

Part Seven

Being Part of the Higher-Self Community

When you first come into a spiritual teaching, it is important to start a routine at home. This consists of meditation in the morning, reading, doing the class work, working with a buddy, and spending social time to get to know the people in the teaching with whom you feel a good relationship.

We talk about community and how important it is. Once you are part of the community, try to expand your social circle and include some of these new relationships.

People who are physically in the same class often socialize together. If you don't have the physical connection in class, it is good to reach out and talk to people either online or on the telephone. Going to a retreat will help you connect with certain people and arrange to continue the connection when you return home.

When you meet someone in the teaching, always privately link your heart to that person and ask your Higher Self if it would be right for you to develop a personal relationship with the person. If the answer you get is no, that usually means there are some hidden components that may come up later and cause a break in the relationship. Remember, karma attracts you to a person initially—whether it is good or bad.

Also, there are people in this teaching who have been together for over twenty years. Some of them have bonded and have very close relationships. If you are with them in a setting other than class, you may feel shunned or left out. Even if they try to include you, you may sense the strong connection between them and feel that somehow you don't belong. Try not to feel excluded. Be open, and when they are welcoming, feel that welcome and not the fact that they are bonded in a way that you aren't. Most people in this teaching really want new people to join and are happy when they do.

If you want to ask advice or confide something to a person with whom you feel close in the teaching, and the person is someone other than a mentor or buddy, please tell him to keep it private—not to mention it to anyone else. In class, and in the buddy work, that privacy is understood. No one reveals what takes place to anyone outside the group or person. Confidentiality is very important in this teaching.

We also have a strict rule of not gossiping about anyone. Since this is a family, things happen that people want to tell one another. Just keep it from becoming gossip. Gossip usually multiplies and gets back to the person. It also can be humiliating and destructive to the person being talked about. If you see something that a person does that you don't like, tell the person directly. Everyone on the spiritual path goes through challenges that can sometimes bring out the worst in him or her. Be helpful if you see this and realize that no one is perfect.

In particular, if the person is someone from your past that caused negative karma, you may find you judge that person more than you would anyone else.

You also may meet someone in the teaching who dislikes you. Again, it has to do with something from your past. Even when you sit down and try to resolve the feeling, it can still come up again during classes or retreats. Sometimes a person may not even be aware of how he is acting toward you.

When that occurs, instead of reacting in a negative manner, the best thing to do is first to realize what is happening and then to throw out any upset from your heart and send the person love. The more you do that, the more the person will let go of his resentment. Do the same if you suddenly feel the same negativity toward someone else—link with your heart, send the negativity out, and send the person love.

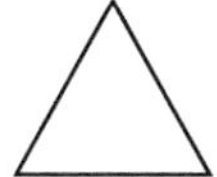

Part Eight

Psychological Work

Higher Self Yoga has a strong psychological component that is a major part of the teaching. I have realized that the main problem most people have on a spiritual path is the inability to overcome some of their psychological problems that were formed in childhood.

Many people who enter a spiritual teaching must pay off difficult karma in their childhood, so they are free to join their destined teaching. This karma often affects who they become as adults and causes them even to continue to suffer from that karma in their adulthood.

In the past, no treatment existed to help people overcome some of the wounds that were suffered. Psychotherapy came into the world in the twentieth century and has become a very important factor for people in this teaching. Because childhood conditioning can cause strong feelings of unworthiness, it is a key factor in stopping people spiritually.

To grow spiritually, you have to have a strong sense of purpose, understanding of others, an inner feeling of loving yourself, and, mainly, the ability to develop leadership skills without fear around power.

A true leader needs self-acceptance and the knowledge of right and wrong. A yogi has to be able to stand up to injustice, feel compassion and love of others, and feel self-assured that she will do her best in any endeavor she starts. If a yogi carries negative feelings about herself, she will not be able to handle strife, conflict, or any situation where she has to be strong, but caring.

Because I feel psychotherapy is important for a yogi to have in order to move forward on the path, I have asked all my students to work on themselves by going to a professional psychotherapist. Some students have resisted doing this, but at a certain point they realized that they were blocked and that it was affecting them spiritually.

No other spiritual teaching has asked this of their students. We aren't requiring it, but we feel it's very important for everyone who wants to grow spiritually to heal any wounds they are carrying with them.

Some of these wounds also come from past lives. In this teaching, students experience and see past lives. This usually happens when someone is at a point in her journey that needs clarification of things she is experiencing or even feeling.

It can also occur when a student needs to understand what is blocking her from moving forward. When a past life starts to come up, then one of our therapists can help the person see the lifetime and come to a deeper understanding of how it has affected her.

We do not encourage people to do past-life work unless it is necessary. It is wrong to try to force it, as it can be overwhelming when someone isn't ready to experience or understand it. We only encourage it when someone is blocked from moving forward. Usually, one of the advanced teachers or I recognize when that would be important. Also, the past-life therapists work with the Higher Self when they do the session to make sure the person is ready to see a former lifetime. If she isn't ready, the Higher Self will indicate as much.

There will be a time when past-life therapy will be part of most psychotherapists' work. This is because many of the characteristics that need healing have often come from karma and past lives.

For example, if someone has been controlling and abusive to others in a past life, the person will come back into a situation where she herself is controlled and abused, causing deep wounds. This can happen time and time again, until the person learns never to continue being controlling or abusive. This is what Buddha called the wheel of karma.

Anyone coming into this teaching, at this time in her evolution, will have paid off most of her karma; otherwise, she wouldn't be ready to enter a spiritual teaching.

There will be a time when the disciple needs to know many of her past lives and recognize all the characteristics that are negative as well as all the characteristics that are positive. This is because to grow spiritually you have to understand who you are, both in this life and from previous lives. That understanding will help you find the real you, or what is sometimes called *the Be-ness within.*

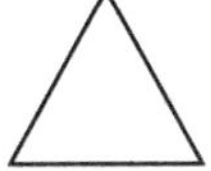

Part Nine

Walking the Path

When you start this journey, you walk what we call *the path*. It is a path full of twists and turns. Sometimes, you will come to an impasse and have to return to where there was a fork in the road and go in the other direction. Other times, you will come to a clearing and experience the beauty that surrounds you.

When you come to a block on the path, stop for a while, realize that the path is still there in front of you, and know that it might take a little while to find it. Know that the path will end on the summit where you will find your ultimate goal.

When you start the journey, do so with the knowledge that you have the tools within to continue. Your heart will always guide you, and your mind will help you to take the right direction. Know that you also have in front of you others who have gone before you and have found the end of the path.

They will always help you when you are entangled in the woods and when you feel unable to cross a stream. They will watch you and understand when you feel lost and discouraged. They are your guardians and will never let you experience harm.

When you start your journey, feel the power of what will happen if you have the faith and the desire to continue. Know that it is a long journey that sometimes will take several lifetimes to complete. Also know that if you are here again starting to walk the path, you have done this before—at least two times and maybe many more.

When you start your journey, feel in your heart that it is worth all the obstacles and all the challenges because it will end in Joy.

When you think about Joy, think about having wisdom; when you feel Joy, know you are experiencing the beautiful. When you seek Joy, know you are forever on a quest that will take you into far-off worlds. When you realize Joy, know you have earned its essence by constant striving toward the light.

Joy is a special wisdom; it cannot come from outside you, only from within you.

www.ingramcontent.com/pod-product-compliance
Lightning Source LLC
LaVergne TN
LVHW010945110826
845149LV00013B/2759

* 9 7 8 0 9 8 9 4 6 8 2 9 9 *